SkillBuilder

Grade 4

English Workbook - 2

▸ *Language*

Complement Classroom Learning All Year

Using the Lumos Study Program, parents and teachers can reinforce the classroom learning experience for children. It creates a collaborative learning platform for students, teachers and parents.

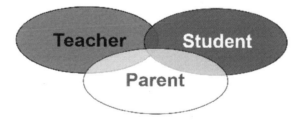

Used in Schools and Libraries To Improve Student Achievement

Lumos Learning
Developed by Expert Teachers

Contributing Author - Mary Evans Rumley
Contributing Author - Julie Turner
Executive Producer - Mukunda Krishnaswamy
Designer - Harini Nagaraj
Database Administrator - Raghavendra Rao R.

ISBN-10: 1-940484-90-1

ISBN-13: 978-1-940484-90-7

Printed in the United States of America

For permissions and additional information contact us

Lumos Information Services, LLC
Email: support@lumoslearning.com

PO Box 1575
Piscataway, NJ 08855-1575
Tel: (732) 384-0146
Fax: (866) 283-6471

http://www.LumosLearning.com

Lumos English Language and Grammar Skill Builder, Grade 4 - Conventions, Vocabulary and Knowledge of Language

This Book Includes:

- Practice questions to help students master
  - Language
- Detailed Answer explanations for every question
- Strategies for building speed and accuracy

Plus access to Online Workbooks which include:

- Instructional videos
- Mobile apps related to the learning objective
- Hundreds of additional practice questions
- Self-paced learning and personalized score reports
- Instant feedback after completion of the workbook

Table of Contents

Introduction

Books in the Lumos Skill Builder series are designed to help students master specific skills in Math and English Language Arts. The content of each workbook is rigorous and aligned with the robust standards. Each standard, and substandard, has its own specific content. Taking the time to study and practice each standard individually can help students more adequately understand and demonstrate proficiency of that standard in their particular grade level.

Unlike traditional printed books, this book provides online access to engaging educational videos, mobile apps and assessments. Blending printed resources with technology based learning tools and resources has proven to be an effective strategy to help students of the current generation master learning objectives. We call these books tedBooks™ since they connect printed books to a repository of online learning resources!

Additionally, students have individual strengths and weaknesses. Being able to practice content by standard allows them the ability to more deeply understand each standard and be able to work to strengthen academic weaknesses. The online resources create personalized learning opportunities for each student and provides immediate individualized feedback.

We believe that yearlong learning and adequate practice before the test are the keys to success on standardized tests. The books in the Skill Builder series will help students gain foundational skills needed to perform well on the standardized tests.

How to Use this Book Effectively

The Lumos Program is a flexible learning tool. It can be adapted to suit a student's skill level and the time available to practice. Here are some tips to help you use this book and the online resources effectively:

Students

- The standards in each book can be practiced in the order designed, or in the order of your own choosing.
- Answer all questions in each workbook.
- Use the online workbooks to further practice your areas of difficulty and complement classroom learning.
- Watch videos recommended for the lesson or question.
- Download and try mobile apps related to what you are learning.

Parents

- Get student reports and useful information about your school by downloading the Lumos SchoolUp™ app. Please follow directions provided in "How to download Lumos SchoolUp™ App" section of this chapter.
- Review your child's performance in the "Lumos Online Workbooks" periodically. You can do this by simply asking your child to log into the system online and selecting the subject area you wish to review.
- Review your child's work in each workbook.

- You can use the Lumos online programs along with this book to complement and extend your classroom instruction.
- Get a Free Teacher account by visiting http://lumoslearning.com/a/fta

This Lumos StepUp® Basic account will help you:

- Create up to 30 student accounts.
- Review the online work of your students.
- Create and share information about your classroom or school events.

NOTE: There is a limit of one grade and subject per teacher for the free account.

- Download the Lumos SchoolUp™ mobile app using the instructions provided in "How can I Download the App?" section of this chapter to conveniently monitor your students online progress.

First Time Access:

Using a personal computer with internet access:	Using a smartphone or tablet:
Go to http://www.lumoslearning.com/a/workbooks	Scan the QR Code below and follow the instructions.
Select your State and enter the following access code in the Access Code field and press the Submit button.	
Access Code: NCG4LG-19621-P	

In the next screen, click on the "Register" button to register your username and password.

Subsequent Access:

After you establish your user id and password for subsequent access, simply login with your account information.

What if I buy more than one Lumos Study Program?

Please note that you can use all Online Workbooks with one User ID and Password. If you buy more than one book, you will access them with the same account.

Go back to the **http://lumoslearning.com/a/workbooks** link and enter the access code provided in the second book. In the next screen simply login using your previously created account.

Lumos StepUp® Mobile App FAQ For Students

What is the Lumos StepUp® App?

It is a FREE application you can download onto your Android smart phones, tablets, iPhones, and iPads.

What are the Benefits of the StepUp® App?

This mobile application gives convenient access to Practice Tests, Common Core State Standards, Online Workbooks, and learning resources through your smart phone and tablet computers.

- Eleven Technology enhanced question types in both MATH and ELA
- Sample questions for Arithmetic drills
- Standard specific sample questions
- Instant access to the Common Core State Standards
- Jokes and cartoons to make learning fun!

Do I Need the StepUp® App to Access Online Workbooks?

No, you can access Lumos StepUp® Online Workbooks through a personal computer. The StepUp® app simply enhances your learning experience and allows you to conveniently access StepUp® Online Workbooks and additional resources through your smart phone or tablet.

How can I Download the App?

Visit **lumoslearning.com/a/stepup-app** using your smart phone or tablet and follow the instructions to download the app.

QR Code
for Smart Phone
Or Tablet Users

Lumos SchoolUp™ Mobile App FAQ For Parents and Teachers

What is the Lumos SchoolUp™ App?

It is a free app that teachers can use to easily access real-time student activity information as well as assign learning resources to students. Parents can also use it to easily access school-related information such as homework assigned by teachers and PTA meetings. It can be downloaded onto smart phones and tablets from popular App Stores.

What are the Benefits of the Lumos SchoolUp™ App?

It provides convenient access to
- Real-time student activity information.
- School "Stickies". A Sticky could be information about an upcoming test, homework, extra curricular activities and other school events. Parents and educators can easily create their own sticky and share with the school community.
- Discover useful educational videos and mobile apps.
- Common Core State Standards.
- Educational blogs.
- StepUp™ student activity reports.

How can I Download the App?

Visit **lumoslearning.com/a/schoolup-app** using your smartphone or tablet and follow the instructions provided to download the App. Alternatively, scan the QR Code provided below using your smartphone or tablet computer.

**QR Code
for Smart Phone
Or Tablet Users**

Language

Question Number: 7

Kelly and I have been going to dances for two years now, but her little sister wants to come with us this time. This is _____ first time at a school dance.

Choose the appropriate pronoun.

Ⓐ her
Ⓑ my
Ⓒ she
Ⓓ it

Question Number: 8

_____ went hiking in the mountains together.

Complete the sentence with the appropriate pronoun.

Ⓐ His
Ⓑ Her
Ⓒ They
Ⓓ Them

Question Number: 9

I baked fancy Christmas cupcakes for my teacher. She is my favorite teacher and I couldn't wait until Monday to give them to _____.

Choose the correct pronoun.

Ⓐ she
Ⓑ him
Ⓒ he
Ⓓ her

Question Number: 10

Alice and Jennifer like going ice skating. _____ are going to the ice skating rink this afternoon.

Choose the correct pronoun.

- Ⓐ Their
- Ⓑ They
- Ⓒ Them
- Ⓓ Her

Online Resources: Pronouns

URL	QR Code
http://lumoslearning.com/a/15123	

 Videos Apps Sample Questions

NOTES

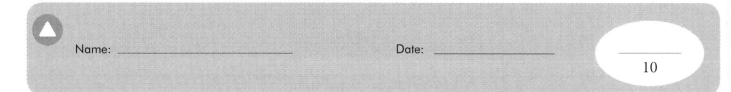
Progressive Verb Tense

Question Number: 1

Efrain, accompanied by his parents, _____ to Europe this summer.
Choose the correct progressive verb tense.

- Ⓐ are traveling
- Ⓑ will be traveling
- Ⓒ was traveling
- Ⓓ is traveling

Question Number: 2

Darrel and I _____ the football game with friends this Friday night.
Choose the correct verb to complete the sentence.

- Ⓐ is attending
- Ⓑ am attending
- Ⓒ was attending
- Ⓓ will attend

Question Number: 3

Choose the sentence that has the proper progressive verb tense.

- Ⓐ Minnie, Jill, and Sandra are singing the birthday song to Ann right now.
- Ⓑ Bob, Jim, and Harry have played baseball next summer.
- Ⓒ One of my five hamsters is getting out of the cage tomorrow night.
- Ⓓ Twenty-five dollars are too much to charge for that bracelet.

Question Number: 4

Choose the sentence that has proper verb tense.

- Ⓐ Everyone in my neighborhood, including the woman with nine dogs, were walking each night after dinner.
- Ⓑ Contestants from Europe, America, and Germany are competing in last year's contest.
- Ⓒ Neither of the girls is planning to audition for the school play today.
- Ⓓ No one in my history class wish that we had more homework each night.

Question Number: 5

Jenny, one of my many friends, _____ to buy a new car this summer with money she earns during this school year at her babysitting job.
Choose the correct one.

Ⓐ will be saving
Ⓑ is saving
Ⓒ am saving
Ⓓ be hoping

Question Number: 6

The cheerleader, who was cheering for her team, wore one of the team's new uniforms.

What should the correct sentence be?

Ⓐ The cheerleader, who was cheering for her team, were dressed in one of the team's new uniforms.
Ⓑ The cheerleader, who was cheering for her team, was wearing one of the team's new uniforms.
Ⓒ The cheerleader, who were cheering for her team, were wearing one of the team's new uniforms.
Ⓓ The cheerleaders, who was cheering for her teams, will be wearing one of the teams new uniforms.

Question Number: 7

The trees that keeps waved in the wind on the side of the street show how forceful the wind is.

What should the correct sentence be?

Ⓐ The trees that waved in the wind on the side of the street show how forceful the wind is.
Ⓑ The trees that will be waving in the wind on the side of the street show how forceful the wind is.
Ⓒ The trees that keep waving in the wind on the side of the street show how forceful the wind is.
Ⓓ The trees that keep waving in the wind on the side of the street shows how forceful the wind is.

14

Question Number: 8

The world change so rapidly that we can hardly keep up.
Choose the correct sentence.

Ⓐ The world will be changing so rapidly that we can hardly keep up.
Ⓑ The world change so rapidly that we can hardly keep up.
Ⓒ The world is changing so rapidly that we can hardly keep up.
Ⓓ The worlds change so rapidly that we can hardly keep up.

Question Number: 9

She sitted at the table by the window when the waiter approached.
Choose the correct sentence.

Ⓐ She sitting at the table by the window.
Ⓑ She was sitting at the table by the window.
Ⓒ She is sitting at the table by the window.
Ⓓ Shes will be sitting at the table by the window.

Question Number: 10

Kenji and Briana _____ at recess when their parents pick them up for their doctor appointments.
Which verb best completes the sentence?

Ⓐ play   Ⓒ will be playing
Ⓑ will play   Ⓓ were playing

NOTES

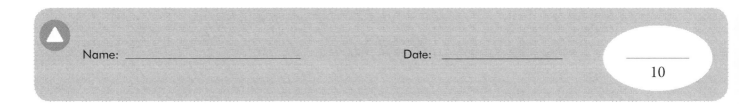
Modal Auxiliary Verbs

Question Number: 1

(1) Rae and her mother need to find a birthday gift for Rae's father, Joseph. (2) They discussed shopping online, walking to the store in their neighborhood, or going to the mall to find the gift. (3) Because Rae's mother suffers from arthritis, I don't think they will walk to the store to buy the gift. (4) They may decide it's most efficient to buy the gift online.

Which sentences contains an auxiliary verb?

Ⓐ sentence 1
Ⓑ sentences 2 and 3
Ⓒ sentence 4
Ⓓ sentences 3 and 4

Question Number: 2

Oliver may go to school tomorrow if his fever has dissipated.

What is the purpose of the modal auxiliary verb, "may," in the sentence?.

Ⓐ It is being used to express doubt.
Ⓑ It is being used to talk about a future event with uncertainty.
Ⓒ It is being used to talk about something that will definitely happen.
Ⓓ It is being used to talk about something that definitely will not happen.

Question Number: 3

Liam can have taken the test before he went on vacation, but he did not inform his teacher about the trip in advance.

Replace "can" with the correct verb in the sentence.

Ⓐ will
Ⓑ must
Ⓒ can't
Ⓓ could

Question Number: 4

Dana had to leave the party when her mother called to inform her of an emergency at home.

What is the auxiliary modal verb in the sentence?

Ⓐ called to
Ⓑ at
Ⓒ had to
Ⓓ will

Question Number: 5

Choose the sentence that contains a modal auxiliary verb.

Ⓐ You shouldn't have handled your disagreement with physical violence.
Ⓑ I want to have a birthday party.
Ⓒ Everyone needs to look up.
Ⓓ That is the most beautiful painting I have ever seen.

Question Number: 6

Choose the sentence that contains a modal auxiliary verb.

Ⓐ You are a very good reader.
Ⓑ Sara is having a great time on her Hawaiian vacation.
Ⓒ I am not a big fan of Justin Beiber.
Ⓓ You could be a really good student if you applied yourself to your studies.

Question Number: 7

Choose the sentence that contains a modal auxiliary verb.

Ⓐ Jerome has potential to be an excellent science fiction writer.
Ⓑ Margaret is the most beautiful dancer on the stage.
Ⓒ I shall never think another bad thought again.
Ⓓ Jenny is eating a sandwich for dinner.

Question Number: 8

(1)If I could dine with any person, living or dead, I would choose Maya Angelou. (2)She endured hardships in her life but went on to become one of the most influential literary figures of the 20th century. (3)I will ask her what inspired her most.

"Will" is not the best verb choice in the 3rd sentence.

What word should the speaker have used instead to express possibility rather than certainty?

Ⓐ can
Ⓑ may
Ⓒ shall
Ⓓ would

Question Number: 9

"Can you hand me that apple?" Marvin asked his mother.
"Yes," she answered. But she didn't move a muscle.

Why did Marvin's mother respond this way?

Ⓐ She had had an extremely long and tiring day at work. Marvin's mother did not want to hand him the apple.
Ⓑ Marvin's mother recognizes she can hand him the apple and knows there is a better way for him to ask using the word "will".
Ⓒ Marvin's mother does not approve of apples.
Ⓓ She thinks Marvin should have to get his own apple.

Question Number: 10

Choose the sentence that correctly uses a modal auxiliary verb.

Ⓐ I might have to see a doctor if this headache does not go away.
Ⓑ I shall all the items on the menu.
Ⓒ She musted remembered to lock the front door before leaving for work each day.
Ⓓ Her might need to go to the school for a conference tomorrow.

NOTES

Adjectives and Adverbs

Question Number: 1

(1) Mary went to visit her grandmother last weekend. (2) She likes to visit her grandmother beautiful frequently. (3) While visiting, they enjoy walking. (4) They strolled in the beautiful park and talked. (5) Mary and her grandmother enjoyed their visit.

Identify the _adverb_ used in _sentence 2_.

Ⓐ likes
Ⓑ visits
Ⓒ frequently
Ⓓ her

Question Number: 2

(1) Mary went to visit her grandmother last weekend. (2) She likes to visit her grandmother frequently. (3) While visiting, they enjoy walking. (4) They strolled in the beautiful park and talked. (5) Mary and her grandmother enjoyed their visit.

Identify the _adjective_ used in _sentence 4_.

Ⓐ strolled
Ⓑ beautiful
Ⓒ park
Ⓓ talked

Question Number: 3

Zelda and her family visited the Jackson Zoo last weekend although it was alarmingly cold and rainy.

Identify an _adjective_ in the above sentence.

Ⓐ last
Ⓑ although
Ⓒ and
Ⓓ cold

Question Number: 4

Zelda and her family visited the Jackson Zoo last weekend although it was rainy, alarmingly and cold.

What is the correct order of words in the sentence?

Ⓐ   Zelda and her family visited the Jackson Zoo last weekend although it was cold alarmingly and rainy.
Ⓑ   Zelda and her family visited the Jackson Zoo last weekend although it was alarmingly cold and rainy.
Ⓒ   Zelda and her family visited the Jackson Zoo last weekend although it was rainy and cold.
Ⓓ   Zelda and her family visited the Jackson Zoo last weekend although it was cold, rainy, and alarmingly.

Question Number: 5

It was determined that James was the _____ runner on our track team.

Choose the correct adjective to complete the above sentence.

Ⓐ   most fast
Ⓑ   fastest
Ⓒ   most fastest
Ⓓ   faster

Question Number: 6

(1) Lindsay, Laine, and John were excited. (2) Each put their things in his or her overnight bag. (3) They were going to spend two nights with Aunt Margaret, and the next night with their Auntie Jo.

What is the adjective in sentence 1?

Ⓐ   John
Ⓑ   Lindsay
Ⓒ   Laine
Ⓓ   excited

Question Number: 7

I think that my daughter is the _____ girl in the world.

Choose the appropriate word for the sentence above.

- Ⓐ   beautifulest
- Ⓑ   beautifuler
- Ⓒ   most beautiful
- Ⓓ   more beautiful

Question Number: 8

The wind was much _____ than it was last weekend.

Choose the correct _comparative adjective_ to complete the above sentence.

- Ⓐ   cold
- Ⓑ   coldest
- Ⓒ   more cold
- Ⓓ   colder

Question Number: 9

While standing at the intersection, I heard a loud noise and turned my head to see the _____ wreck imaginable.

Choose the proper comparative adjective to complete the above sentence.

- Ⓐ   horrificest
- Ⓑ   most horrificest
- Ⓒ   more horrificest
- Ⓓ   most horrific

Question Number: 10

The huge tiger hungrily stealthily walked in the black, spiky bush getting ready to pounce.

What's the correct order of adverbs in the sentence above?

Ⓐ Huge, spiky
Ⓑ Hungrily and stealthily
Ⓒ Stealthily and hungrily
Ⓓ Black spiky

Online Resources: Adjectives and Adverbs

URL	QR Code
http://lumoslearning.com/a/15124	

 Videos   Apps   Sample Questions

NOTES

Prepositional Phrases

Question Number: 1

Choose the sentence that contains a prepositional phrase.

Ⓐ The monkey was washing its paws.
Ⓑ The lion jumped into the pool of cool water.
Ⓒ That is the most beautiful dog I have ever seen.
Ⓓ When you decide, let me know.

Question Number: 2

You will find the new notebooks underneath the journals.
Identify the *prepositional phrase* in the above sentence.

Ⓐ will find
Ⓑ notebooks underneath
Ⓒ new notebooks
Ⓓ underneath the journals

Question Number: 3

Choose the sentence that contains a prepositional phrase.

Ⓐ Please put your paper down so that others won't see your answers.
Ⓑ Because he doesn't have enough money to buy ice cream, he must do without.
Ⓒ Do not leave for school without your lunch box.
Ⓓ Please don't forget to let the dog in.

Question Number: 4

Choose the sentence that contains a prepositional phrase.

Ⓐ When entering the room, Ana tripped on the rug and fell.
Ⓑ I want to see the Rocky Mountains.
Ⓒ Everyone needs to look up.
Ⓓ That is the most beautiful painting I have ever seen.

Question Number: 5

Finding his money, Lee and Jose rushed to join their friends at the fair.

Identify the prepositional phrase in the above sentence.

Ⓐ finding his money
Ⓑ rushed to join
Ⓒ their friends
Ⓓ at the fair

Question Number: 6

Identify the sentence that contains two prepositional phrases.

Ⓐ Terrance went into the room to get his book.
Ⓑ Terrance went into the room.
Ⓒ Terrance went into the room and sat in his favorite chair.
Ⓓ Terrance sat in his favorite chair to read.

Question Number: 7

The puppy barked loudly and chased the kitten across the yard.
Identify the prepositional phrase in the above sentence.

Ⓐ barked loudly
Ⓑ chased across
Ⓒ barked loudly and chased
Ⓓ across the yard

Question Number: 8

Identify the sentence that contains a prepositional phrase.

Ⓐ The intoxicating aroma filled the air.
Ⓑ The aroma coming from the kitchen was inviting.
Ⓒ I forgot to purchase a loaf of bread.
Ⓓ A lovely young woman watched as the band marched.

Question Number: 9

Identify the sentence that DOES NOT contains a prepositional phrase.

Ⓐ Are you going to let him answer the question?
Ⓑ The answer to the question was wrong.
Ⓒ The teacher put a huge red checkmark on my paper.
Ⓓ The questions on this test were very difficult.

Question Number: 10

The fox chased the deer down the trail.
Identify the prepositional phrase in the sentence above.

Ⓐ chased the deer
Ⓑ the fox
Ⓒ down the trail
Ⓓ the deer down

Online Resources: Prepositional Phrases

URL	QR Code

http://lumoslearning.com/a/15126

 Videos   Apps   Sample Questions

NOTES

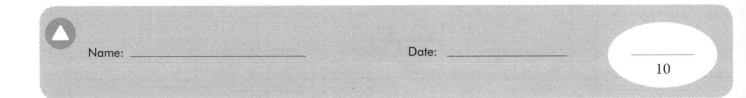
Complete Sentences

Question Number: 1

Jordan wants to go outside and play with her neighbor her mother said she had to clean up her room first.
Which answer choice corrects this run-on sentence?

Ⓐ Jordan wants to go outside and play with her neighbor, but her mother said she had to clean up her room first.

Ⓑ Jordan wants to go outside and play but her mother won't let her.

Ⓒ Jordan wants, to go outside and play with her neighbor but her nother said she had to clean up her room first.

Ⓓ Jordan wants to go outside. And play with her neighbor. But her mother said she had to clean up her room first.

Question Number: 2

George Washington Carver is best known for his work with peanuts but he also taught his students about crop rotation that's when farmers plant different crops each year to avoid draining the soil of its nutrients.
Which answer choice corrects the run-on sentence above?

Ⓐ George Washington Carver is best known for his work with peanuts, but he also taught his students about crop rotation, that's when farmers plant different crops each year to avoid draining the soil of its nutrients

Ⓑ George Washington Carver is best known for his work with peanuts, but he also taught his students about crop rotation. That's when farmers plant different crops each year to avoid draining the soil of its nutrients.

Ⓒ George Washington Carver is best known for his work with peanuts. But he also taught his students about crop rotation. That's when farmers plant different crops each year to avoid draining the soil of its nutrients

Ⓓ George Washington Carver is best known for his work with peanuts but he also taught his students about crop rotation that's when farmers plant different crops each year to avoid draining the soil of its nutrients

Question Number: 3

Which answer choice is a fragment, rather than a complete sentence?

(A) Be careful what you wish for.
(B) He should not run with scissors.
(C) If you can't say something nice.
(D) Don't say anything at all.

Question Number: 4

Three ways to transfer heat.
What would transform this fragment into a complete sentence?

(A) Replacing the period with a question mark at the end of the sentence
(B) Adding "convection, conduction, and radiation" to the end of the sentence.
(C) Adding "There are" to the beginning of the sentence.
(D) Nothing. The sentence is complete already.

Question Number: 5

(1)Producers make their own food from the sun during a process called photosynthesis. (2)The Greek root, "photo," means "light." (3)Means "to put together." (4)So "photosynthesis" means "to put together with light," which is exactly what plants do when they make their own food.
Which sentence is a fragment, rather than a complete sentence?

(A) Sentence 1
(B) Sentence 2
(C) Sentence 3
(D) Sentence 4

Question Number: 6

(1)Jawaad held his head high. (2)As he strode to the front of the classroom to present his research report. (3)The report compared the Norse god, Thor, to the Marvel Comic version of Thor. (4)He was proud of his work and thought the class would really enjoy it.

Choose the best edited version of the above paragraph. Pay attention to run-on sentences and fragments.

Ⓐ   Jawaad held his head high. As he strode to the front of the classroom to present his research report. The report compared the Norse god, Thor, to the Marvel Comic version of Thor. He was proud of the work and thought the class would really enjoyed it.

Ⓑ   Jawaad held his head high. As he strode to the front of the classroom to present his research report, the report compared the Norse god, Thor, to the Marvel Comic version of Thor. He was proud of the work and thought the class would really enjoyed it.

Ⓒ   Jawaad held his head high. As he strode to the front of the classroom to present his research report. The report compared the Norse god, Thor, to the Marvel Comic version of Thor he was proud of the work and thought the class would really enjoyed it.

Ⓓ   Jawaad held his head high as he strode to the front of the classroom to present his research report. The report compared the Norse god, Thor, to the Marvel Comic version of Thor. He was proud of the work and thought the class would really enjoyed it.

Question Number: 7

Choose the run-on sentence.

Ⓐ   Felix has a mischievous spirit he is somehow quite well-behaved.
Ⓑ   Margaret is the most beautiful dancer on the stage.
Ⓒ   The sky was the limit for a bright, energetic, young prodigy like Ben.
Ⓓ   None of the above

Question Number: 8

(1)If I could dine with any person, living or dead, I would choose Maya Angelou. (2)She endured hardships in her life but went on to become one of the most influential literary figures of the 20th century. (3)I would ask her what inspired her most.

Identify the run-on sentence.

Ⓐ   Sentence 1
Ⓑ   Sentence 2
Ⓒ   Sentence 3
Ⓓ   None of the above

Question Number: 9

A really great pair of shoes.
What would transform the fragment into a complete sentence?

Ⓐ A really great pair of shoes, two ironed shirts, and two pairs of dress pants.
Ⓑ A really great pair of shoes should be both stylish and comfortable.
Ⓒ Doesn't need a really great pair of shoes.
Ⓓ My friend's really great pair of shoes.

Question Number: 10

Choose the complete sentence.

Ⓐ While she is a very sweet puppy, I can't justify adopting her.
Ⓑ While she is a very sweet puppy.
Ⓒ Because my apartment is too small.
Ⓓ I can't justify adopting this puppy my apartment is too small.

NOTES

Frequently Confused Words

Question Number: 1

Divya and her family celebrate Diwali, a traditional festival in _____ culture.
Choose the correct word to complete the sentence.

Ⓐ their
Ⓑ they're
Ⓒ there
Ⓓ the're

Question Number: 2

Place your projects over _____ until it's time to present.
Choose the correct word to complete the sentence.

Ⓐ their
Ⓑ they're
Ⓒ there
Ⓓ the're

Question Number: 3

Gretchen and Laura are thankful _____ able to peer edit each other's writing.
Choose the correct word to complete the sentence.

Ⓐ their
Ⓑ they're.
Ⓒ there
Ⓓ the're

Question Number: 4

We're going too my grandmother's house for Thanksgiving, but we'll be driving back home on Friday.
Choose the best edited version of the sentence.

Ⓐ We're going two my grandmother's house for Thanksgiving, but we'll be driving back home on Friday.
Ⓑ Were going too my grandmother's house for Thanksgiving, but we'll be driving back home on Friday.
Ⓒ We're going to my grandmother's house for Thanksgiving, but we'll be driving back home on Friday.
Ⓓ The sentence is correct already.

Question Number: 5

I assumed the mall would be crowded today. Were are all the people?
What error did the writer make?

Ⓐ She wrote a run-on sentence.
Ⓑ She spelled "assumed" incorrectly.
Ⓒ She used "were" instead of "where."
Ⓓ She wrote a fragment.

Question Number: 6

We don't have any milk or bread, so _____ going to the grocery store right this instant.
Which word best completes the sentence?

Ⓐ **were**
Ⓑ **we're**
Ⓒ **where**
Ⓓ **there**

Question Number: 7

I can't take another breathe until I know how this book will end.
What error did the writer make?

Ⓐ She should have used the word, "breath," rather than "breathe."
Ⓑ She should never hold her breath because she could faint.
Ⓒ She should have used "took," rather than "take."
Ⓓ She should have used "an other" instead of "another."

Question Number: 8

Amal _____ his exam with flying colors. He knew it was because he studied so hard.
Choose the correct word to complete the sentence.

Ⓐ pessed
Ⓑ pest
Ⓒ past
Ⓓ passed

Question Number: 9

I have to _____ that science does not come easily for me. If I want to do well I will have to work at it.
Choose the correct word to complete the sentence.

Ⓐ except
Ⓑ accept
Ⓒ expect
Ⓓ exccept

Question Number: 10

Choose the correct sentence.

Ⓐ We base our school rules around the common principal that everyone should be treated with respect.
Ⓑ The principal called Evelyn to her office to reward her for perfect attendance.
Ⓒ Jamar was extatic when he was chosen as a principle dancer in the ballet.
Ⓓ Kelsey became the most principaled person at the school.

NOTES

How is it Capitalized?

Question Number: 1

Although spring and summer are my favorite seasons, our family gathering on thanksgiving makes november my favorite month.
Identify the words that need to be capitalized in the above sentence.

Ⓐ Spring, November
Ⓑ Thanksgiving, November
Ⓒ Summer, Thanksgiving
Ⓓ Seasons, November

Question Number: 2

<u>dr. j. howard smith</u>
1141 east palm street
washington, la 98654
Correctly capitalize the underlined portion of the above address.

Ⓐ Dr. J. Howard Smith
Ⓑ DR. J. Howard Smith
Ⓒ Dr. J. howard smith
Ⓓ Dr. j. Howard Smith

Question Number: 3

dr. j. howard smith
<u>1141 east palm street</u>
washington, la 98654
Correctly capitalize the underlined portion of the above address.

Ⓐ 1141 east Palm Street
Ⓑ 1141 East palm Street
Ⓒ 1141 east palm Street
Ⓓ 1141 East Palm Street

Question Number: 4

dr. j. howard smith
1141 east palm street
<u>washington, la 98654</u>
Correctly capitalize the underlined portion of the above address.

Ⓐ Washington, LA 98654
Ⓑ Washington, La 98654
Ⓒ washington, LA 98654
Ⓓ washington, La 98654

Question Number: 5

Next Semester, I plan to take English, History, Math, Spanish, and Music.

Edit the above sentence for capitalization. Choose the sentence that is written correctly.

Ⓐ Next Semester, I plan to take English, History, Spanish, and music.
Ⓑ Next semester, I plan to take English, History, Spanish, and Music.
Ⓒ Next semester, I plan to take english, history, spanish, and music.
Ⓓ Next semester, I plan to take English, history, Spanish, and music.

Question Number: 6

In Mrs. Hart's English class, we are reading <u>the indian in the cupboard</u>.

Choose the title of the book that has correct capitalization.

Ⓐ <u>The Indian In The Cupboard</u>
Ⓑ <u>The Indian in the Cupboard</u>
Ⓒ <u>The indian in the Cupboard</u>
Ⓓ <u>the Indian in the Cupboard</u>

Question Number: 7

The entire family is excited and looking forward to our visit with aunt jenny, my uncle, my grandfather, and grandma.

Choose the correctly capitalized version of the above sentence.

Ⓐ The entire Family is excited and looking forward to our visit with Aunt jenny, my uncle, my grandfather, and Grandma.

Ⓑ The entire family is excited and looking forward to our visit with Aunt jenny, my uncle, my Grandfather, and Grandma.

Ⓒ The entire family is excited and looking forward to our visit with Aunt Jenny, my uncle, my grandfather, and Grandma.

Ⓓ The entire family is excited and looking forward to our visit with aunt Jenny, my Uncle, my Grandfather, and Grandma.

Question Number: 8

yours truly,
timmy newlin

Choose correctly capitalized version of the above letter closing.

Ⓐ Yours Truly,
Timmy Newlin

Ⓑ yours truly,
Timmy Newlin

Ⓒ Yours truly,
Timmy Newlin

Ⓓ Yours truly,
Timmy newlin

Question Number: 9

the chicago river runs into the mississippi valley waterways.

Which words should be capitalized?

Ⓐ The, Chicago
Ⓑ The, Chicago River
Ⓒ The, Chicago River, Mississippi
Ⓓ The, Chicago River, Mississippi Valley

Question Number: 10

I love these lime green nike shoes that my grandma got me for my birthday.

Which word in the above sentence should be capitalized?

Ⓐ Grandma
Ⓑ Birthday
Ⓒ Nike
Ⓓ Shoes

Online Resources: How is it Capitalized?

URL	QR Code
http://lumoslearning.com/a/15128	

 Videos   Apps   Sample Questions

NOTES

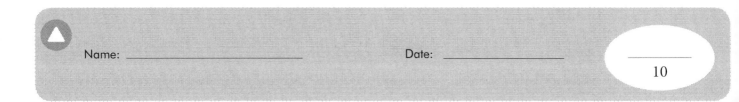
What's the Punctuation?

Question Number: 1

Choose the sentence that is punctuated correctly.

Ⓐ Before I go to bed each night I brush my teeth.
Ⓑ The rabbit scampered across the yard, and ran into the woods.
Ⓒ I don't like to watch scary movies but I like to read scary books.
Ⓓ Our teacher gave us time to study before she gave us the test.

Question Number: 2

Choose the sentence that correctly punctuates a quotation.

Ⓐ "Did you remember to lock the door," asked Jenny?
Ⓑ "Did you remember to lock the door? asked Jenny."
Ⓒ Jenny asked "Did you remember to lock the door?"
Ⓓ Jenny asked, "Did you remember to lock the door?"

Question Number: 3

Choose the sentence that contains a punctuation error.

Ⓐ Cindy wants to go to the mall this afternoon, but her mother will not let her.
Ⓑ Wendy stayed up all night completing her science project, but forgot to take it with her.
Ⓒ Henry forgot to close the gate securely, so his dog escaped from the backyard.
Ⓓ Jimmy and John joined the Army; Billy and George joined the Navy.

Question Number: 4

Do you know Shel Silverstein's poem The Boa Constrictor our teacher asked.

What is the correct way to write the sentence above?

Ⓐ "Do you know Shel Silverstein's poem 'The Boa Constrictor'?" our teacher asked.
Ⓑ "Do you know Shel Silverstein's poem "The Boa Constrictor"? our teacher asked.
Ⓒ "Do you know Shel Silverstein's poem The Boa Constrictor"? our teacher asked.
Ⓓ "Do you know Shel Silverstein's poem The Boa Constrictor" she asked?

Question Number: 5

Of all the poems in his latest book she said this is my favorite. It's really very funny she added.

What is the correct way to write the sentence above?

Ⓐ "Of all the poems in his latest book" she said "this is my favorite." "It's really very funny she added."

Ⓑ "Of all the poems in his latest book," she said, "this is my favorite. It's really very funny," she added.

Ⓒ "Of all the poems in his latest book she said this is my favorite. It's really very funny she added."

Ⓓ "Of all the poems in his latest book," she said "this is my favorite. "It's really very funny" she added.

Question Number: 6

Tom's English professor asked him what was wrong.

What is the correct way to write the sentence above?

Ⓐ The sentence is correct.

Ⓑ Tom's English professor asked him "what was wrong?".

Ⓒ "Tom's English professor asked him what was wrong."

Ⓓ Tom's English professor, asked him, what was wrong.

Question Number: 7

Choose the sentence that is punctuated correctly.

Ⓐ Machiavelli's <u>The Prince</u> begins, "All states, all powers, that have held and hold rule over men have been and are either republics or principalities." [public domain text]

Ⓑ machiavelli's <u>The Prince</u> begins, All states, all powers, that have held and hold rule over men have been and are either republics or principalities.

Ⓒ Machiavelli's <u>The Prince</u> begins "All states, all powers, that have held and hold rule over men have been and are either republics or principalities."

Ⓓ Machiavelli's <u>The Prince</u> begins all states, all powers, that have held and hold rule over men have been and are either republics or principalities.

Question Number: 8

Choose the sentence that is punctuated correctly. [from Peter Pan- public domain]

Ⓐ J.M. Barrie wrote all children, except one, grow up.
Ⓑ J.M. Barrie wrote, All children, except one, grow up.
Ⓒ J.M. Barrie wrote, "All children, except one, grow up."
Ⓓ J.M. Barrie wrote "All children, except one, grow up"

Question Number: 9

Choose the sentence that is punctuated correctly.

Ⓐ In his book, *Peter Pan*, J.M. Barrie says Wendy, knew that she must grow up.
Ⓑ In his book, *Peter Pan*, J.M. Barrie says Wendy "knew that she must grow up."
Ⓒ In his book, *Peter Pan*, J.M. Barrie says wendy, "knew that she must grow up
Ⓓ In his book, *Peter Pan*, J.M. Barrie says Wendy, "knew that she must grow up."

Question Number: 10

Choose the sentence that is punctuated correctly.

Ⓐ The snake was long black and scaly.
Ⓑ The snake slithered across the kitchen floor and Tiffany ran to her bedroom to get away.
Ⓒ I don't like to watch scary movies but I like to read scary books.
Ⓓ The snake slithered across the kitchen floor, and Tiffany ran to her bedroom to get away.

Online Resources: What's the Punctuation

URL	QR Code
http://lumoslearning.com/a/15129	

 Videos   Apps   Sample Questions

NOTES

How is it Spelled?

Question Number: 1

Vargas asked his partner, "Could you please _____ your question to make it easier to understand?"
Choose the correctly spelled work that best completes the sentence.

Ⓐ clearify
Ⓑ Clerify
Ⓒ carefully
Ⓓ clarify

Question Number: 2

Find the misspelled word.

Ⓐ ostrich
Ⓑ vehicel
Ⓒ wings
Ⓓ horse

Question Number: 3

Which of the following words are spelled correctly?

Ⓐ Pollution
Ⓑ Polution
Ⓒ Plloution
Ⓓ Polltion

Question Number: 4

Mom asked the mayor, "Do you beleive in ghosts?"
Choose the word that is incorrectly spelled in the above sentence.

Ⓐ asked
Ⓑ mayor
Ⓒ beleive
Ⓓ ghosts

Question Number: 5

Choose the word that is correctly spelled.

(A) monkies
(B) strawberrys
(C) cherrys
(D) donkeys

Question Number: 6

Nicky set the table for dinner, but she forgot to place knifes at each place setting.
Choose that word that is incorrectly spelled in the above sentence.

(A) dinner
(B) knifes
(C) setting
(D) table

Question Number: 7

Choose the word that is NOT spelled correctly.

(A) Collaterol
(B) Enthusiasm
(C) Infrequently
(D) Vigorous

Question Number: 8

Choose the sentence with the misspelled word.

(A) Rosemary skipped across the room to give her grandfather a hug.
(B) I bought a beautiful new aquarium for my goldfish while at the flea market.
(C) After tripping in the cafeteria and spilling her tray, Mary ran from the room crying.
(D) When I opened the box, I realized that the attachment I wanted was sold seperately and not included in the package.

Question Number: 9

Choose the sentence that contains a misspelled word.

Ⓐ Our class just completed a study on the lifecycle of butterflies.
Ⓑ The delivery man stacked the packages and boxxes in his truck.
Ⓒ The turtle jumped from its log, creating quite a splash.
Ⓓ When firefighters were able to contain the flames, the crowd cheered.

Question Number: 10

Which word below is spelled correctly?

Ⓐ nerrate
Ⓑ nihrayt
Ⓒ narrete
Ⓓ narrate

Online Resources: How is it Spelled?

URL	QR Code
http://lumoslearning.com/a/15130	

 Videos   Apps   Sample Questions

NOTES

Word Choice: Attending to Precision

Question Number: 1

Alexander _____ into the living room to show off his new suit. He had a very high opinion of himself!
Choose the word that best completes the sentence.

Ⓐ walked
Ⓑ strutted
Ⓒ trudged
Ⓓ waddled

Question Number: 2

Collecting the garbage was _____ work, but Tom was happy to do it. The job wore on his body, especially during the hottest days of summer, but he knew he was providing an important public service to his community.
Choose the word that best completes the sentence.

Ⓐ uncomfortable
Ⓑ grueling
Ⓒ bad
Ⓓ stupid

Question Number: 3

Dante was _____ about his award for most improved swimmer. He had never wanted anything more!
Choose the word that best completes sentence.

Ⓐ peaceful
Ⓑ happy
Ⓒ elated
Ⓓ disappointed

Question Number: 4

The baby babbled sweetly, making it difficult for her mother to be upset about the _____ mess she had made when she threw spaghetti all over the kitchen.
Choose the word that best completes the sentence.

Ⓐ gigantic
Ⓑ big
Ⓒ wide
Ⓓ deep

Question Number: 5

The defendant's fingerprint at the scene of the crime was the most _____ evidence in the trial. The jury had no choice but to convict her.
Choose the word that best completes the sentence.

Ⓐ worst
Ⓑ damaging
Ⓒ bad
Ⓓ wonderful

Question Number: 6

Shelby was a _____. She was fiesty, and she did not let anyone push her around.
Choose the word that best completes the sentence.

Ⓐ ham
Ⓑ scrooge
Ⓒ shrinking violet
Ⓓ fireball

Question Number: 7

The girls _____ to the front of the crowd to get a glimpse of their favorite boy band.
Choose the word that best completes the sentence.

Ⓐ walked
Ⓑ skipped
Ⓒ dove
Ⓓ clambered

Question Number: 8

Anne is paying attention to choosing precise words in her writing. Which sentence should she use in her personal narrative to describe the overflowing bathtub?

Ⓐ The water <u>dripping</u> over the edge reminded her of a waterfall.
Ⓑ The water <u>spraying</u> over the edge reminded her of a waterfall.
Ⓒ The water <u>bubbling</u> over the edge reminded her of a waterfall.
Ⓓ The water <u>cascading</u> over the edge reminded her of a waterfall.

Question Number: 9

Riley is paying attention to choosing precise words in his writing. Which sentence should he use to help persuade the reader to recycle?

Ⓐ Recycling <u>cuts down on</u> the amount of waste that goes into landfills each year.
Ⓑ Recycling <u>helps us put a little bit less</u> waste into landfills each year.
Ⓒ Recycling <u>reduces</u> the amount of waste that goes into landfills each year.
Ⓓ Recycling <u>makes us put not as much</u> waste into landfills each year.

Question Number: 10

Janet _____ with delight when she called her mother to say she had been accepted to her top choice college.
Choose the word that best completes the sentence.

Ⓐ squealed
Ⓑ spoke
Ⓒ sneezed
Ⓓ growled

NOTES

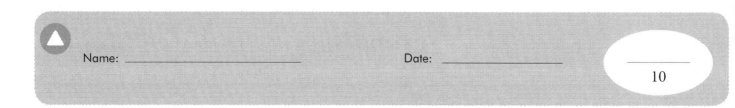
Punctuating for Effect!

Question Number: 1

Jermaine mother said you have to clean your room.
Choose the puntuation that means Jermain's mother is speaking to him.

Ⓐ   Jermaine mother said you have to clean your room.
Ⓑ   "Jermaine, Mother said you have to clean your room."
Ⓒ   Jermaine Mother said, "You have to clean your room."
Ⓓ   "Jermaine," Mother said, "you have to clean your room."

Question Number: 2

Jermaine mother said you have to clean your room.
Choose the puntuation that means a third character is shouting at Jermaine to tell him his mother said to clean his room.

Ⓐ   "Jermaine," Mother said, "you have to clean your room!"
Ⓑ   "Jermaine, Mother said you have to clean your room!"
Ⓒ   "Jermaine," Mother said, "you have to clean your room?"
Ⓓ   "Jermaine, Mother said you have to clean your room."

Question Number: 3

Dante was elated about his award for most improved swimmer. He had never wanted anything more
Choose the most appropriate end punctuation.

Ⓐ   .
Ⓑ   ?
Ⓒ   !
Ⓓ $

Question Number: 4

Choose the sentence that is punctuated correctly.

Ⓐ   The tiger crept carefully through the jungle?
Ⓑ   The tiger crept carefully through the jungle!
Ⓒ   The tiger crept carefully through the jungle
Ⓓ   The tiger crept carefully through the jungle.

Question Number: 5

James was furious when Gemma squirted ketchup all over his new white shirt(1) Sheesh (2) What did Gemma expect to happen (3)
Choose the appropriate end punctuation for sentence 1.

Ⓐ .
Ⓑ !
Ⓒ ?
Ⓓ *

Question Number: 6

James was furious when Gemma squirted ketchup all over his new white shirt(1) Sheesh (2) What did Gemma expect to happen (3)
Choose the appropriate end punctuation for sentence 2.

Ⓐ .
Ⓑ !
Ⓒ ?
Ⓓ *

Question Number: 7

James was furious when Gemma squirted ketchup all over his new white shirt(1) Sheesh (2) What did Gemma expect to happen (3)
Choose the appropriate end punctuation for sentence 3.

Ⓐ .
Ⓑ !
Ⓒ ?
Ⓓ *

Question Number: 8

Wow( ) I can't believe I am going to compete in the national chess competition for my age group!

Which punctuation best follows "Wow"?

Ⓐ .
Ⓑ !
Ⓒ ?
Ⓓ &

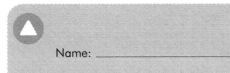
Question Number: 9

Which of the following sentences is NOT punctuated correctly?

Ⓐ Gee whiz!
Ⓑ I can't believe my good fortune!
Ⓒ Why does water evaporate faster when the sun is out!
Ⓓ Clean your room this instant!

Question Number: 10

Which of the following sentences is punctuated correctly?

Ⓐ She startled me when she jumped out of the bushes!
Ⓑ I'm so hungry I'm afraid I won't make it to lunch?
Ⓒ Our teacher is an amazing #storyteller
Ⓓ This is my favorite time of year, "Jenny said."

NOTES

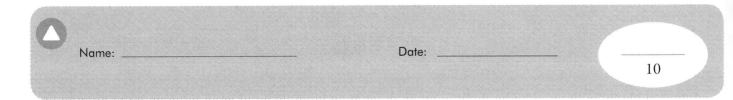
Finding the Meaning

Question Number: 1

The milk is extracted from the coconut, which is used to prepare a variety of dishes and sweets.

What does the word _extracted_ mean in the above sentence?

Ⓐ To put in
Ⓑ To take out of something
Ⓒ To make
Ⓓ To throw out

Question Number: 2

The poor woman was despondent after losing everything she owned in the fire.

Using context clues from the above sentence, the word _despondent_ means:

Ⓐ excited
Ⓑ questioning
Ⓒ despairing
Ⓓ radiant

Question Number: 3

My father tried to console me after my dog died, but nothing he did made me feel better.

Based on the above sentence, console means:

Ⓐ entertain
Ⓑ comfort
Ⓒ talk to
Ⓓ explain

Question Number: 4

The sleepy kittens crawled into bed with their mother. They quickly nestled cozily beside her and went to sleep.

The word _nestled_ means:

- Ⓐ purred softly
- Ⓑ lay down
- Ⓒ leaned against
- Ⓓ snuggled up to

Question Number: 5

Larry gawked in wide-eyed astonishment at the woman wearing the glass hat with fish swimming in it.
Based on the above sentence, the best meaning for the word _gawked_ is:

- Ⓐ glanced at
- Ⓑ stared stupidly
- Ⓒ laughed at
- Ⓓ yelled at

Question Number: 6

If the talking does not cease immediately, you will have 50 additional math problems for home-work.
The word _cease_ means:

- Ⓐ become less noisy
- Ⓑ continue
- Ⓒ decrease
- Ⓓ stop

Question Number: 7

The young men rode their bikes 60 miles to the fair. They did not stop for a break the entire trip. Once they arrived, they were too <u>weary</u> to walk around and enjoy the rides, so they simply lounged on the bleachers and watched the quilt judging.

The word weary means:

Ⓐ excited
Ⓑ tired
Ⓒ energized
Ⓓ enthusiastic

Question Number: 8

The young men rode their bikes 60 miles to the fair. They did not stop for a break the entire trip. Once they arrived, they were too weary to walk around and enjoy the ride, so they simply lounged on the bleachers and watched the quilt judging.

The word _lounged_ means:

Ⓐ watched
Ⓑ sat rigidly
Ⓒ stood
Ⓓ relaxed

Question Number: 9

At the football game Friday night, Bill broke his leg when he plummeted to the ground from the top of the bleachers.

Based on the context clues in the above sentence, the best meaning of the word _plummeted_ is:

Ⓐ floated
Ⓑ drifted
Ⓒ slipped
Ⓓ plunged

Question Number: 10

The weather man is predicting several days of frigid temperatures in the mountains. After watching the weather report, I decided to pack thermal shirts and pants, wool sweaters, gloves, and my warmest coat for the camping trip this weekend.

According to the sentence above, the word _frigid_ means:

Ⓐ rising
Ⓑ freezing
Ⓒ warm
Ⓓ chilly

Online Resources: Finding the Meanings

URL	QR Code

http://lumoslearning.com/a/15131

 Videos   Apps   Sample Questions

NOTES

Context Clues

Question Number: 1

Franklin D. Roosevelt gave his first inaugural address in 1933, during the midst of the Great Depression. He famously said, "The only thing we have to fear is... fear itself." His <u>sentiment</u> helped assuage the fears of many Americans, giving them hope for better days ahead.

What is the meaning of the word, "sentiment," in the paragraph above?

Ⓐ a person who often cries
Ⓑ a view or attitude toward a situation or event
Ⓒ a nice piece of jewelry
Ⓓ blame

Question Number: 2

Franklin D. Roosevelt gave his first inaugural address in 1933, during the midst of the Great Depression. He famously said, "The only thing we have to fear is... fear itself." This sentiment helped <u>assuage</u> the fears of many Americans, giving them hope for better days ahead.

What is the meaning of the word, "assuage," in the paragraph above?

Ⓐ to make worse
Ⓑ to ease
Ⓒ to heighten
Ⓓ to strengthen

Question Number: 3

The restaurant catered to an <u>affluent</u> crowd. The food was very expensive, the tablecloths were crisp and white, and patrons were expected to dress nicely.

What is the meaning of the word, "affluent," in the paragraph above?

Ⓐ practical
Ⓑ wealthy
Ⓒ honest
Ⓓ poor

Question Number: 4

The restaurant catered to an affluent crowd. The food was very expensive, the tablecloths were crisp and white, and <u>patrons</u> were expected to dress nicely in order to eat there.

What is the meaning of the word, "patrons," in the paragraph above?

Ⓐ doctors
Ⓑ waiters
Ⓒ cooks
Ⓓ customers

Question Number: 5

In Charles Dickens's classic tale, Ebenezer Scrooge is a <u>miser</u>-- someone who wishes to spend as little money as possible. As a result, his life is devoid of any meaningful relationships with other people. He does not have any true friends to speak of.

In the paragraph above, what is the meaning of the word, "miser?"

Ⓐ someone who gives gifts often
Ⓑ someone who wishes to spend as little money as possible
Ⓒ someone who thinks of others before themselves
Ⓓ someone who is very old

Question Number: 6

In Charles Dickens's classic tale, Ebenezer Scrooge is a miser-- someone who wishes to spend as little money as possible. As a result, his life is <u>devoid</u> of any meaningful relationships with other people. He does not have any true friends to speak of.

In the paragraph above, what is the meaning of the word, "devoid?"

Ⓐ blooming
Ⓑ decorated
Ⓒ filled with
Ⓓ lacking entirely

Question Number: 7

The hospital <u>corridor</u> was long and cold. Door after door opened into room after room of patients in various stages of rest and recovery. Hazel was earnest in her desire to bring some degree of joy to each of them. That's what clowns are for, after all!

What is the meaning of the word, "corridor," in the paragraph above?

Ⓐ bed
Ⓑ room
Ⓒ desk
Ⓓ hallway

Question Number: 8

The hospital corridor was long and cold. Door after door opened into room after room of patients in various stages of rest and recovery. Hazel was <u>earnest</u> in her desire to bring some degree of joy to each of them. That's what clowns are for, after all!

What is the meaning of the word, "earnest," in the paragraph above?

Ⓐ willing
Ⓑ excited
Ⓒ money that shows serious intent to do a deal
Ⓓ a serious and intent mental state

Question Number: 9

Marcus decided to <u>invest</u> in Mel and Deena's lemonade stand. He gave them twenty dollars to buy fresh lemons, cups, and sugar. In return Mel and Deena will reimburse him with money they earn selling the lemonade plus ten percent of each cup they sell.

In the paragraph above, what is the meaning of the word, "invest?"

Ⓐ to really enjoy lemonade
Ⓑ to cheer someone one by clapping and shouting
Ⓒ to give someone money for fun
Ⓓ to give someone money with hopes of making money

Question Number: 10

Marcus decided to invest in Mel and Deena's lemonade stand. He gave them twenty dollars to buy fresh lemons, cups, and sugar. In return Mel and Deena will <u>reimburse</u> him with money they earn selling the lemonade plus ten percent of each cup they sell.

In the paragraph above, what is the meaning of the word, "reimburse."

Ⓐ to repay
Ⓑ to hit
Ⓒ to shower
Ⓓ to take

NOTES

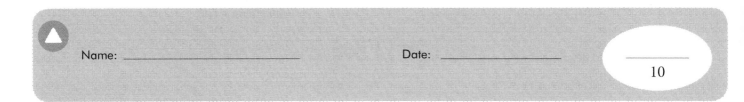
The Meaning of Words

Question Number: 1

Mindy was surprised to discover how disorganized the students had left the books. What is the meaning of the word <u>disorganized</u>?

Ⓐ organized
Ⓑ not organized
Ⓒ neat
Ⓓ torn

Question Number: 2

Which of the following words contains a prefix that means <u>again</u>?

Ⓐ preview
Ⓑ international
Ⓒ rewind
Ⓓ disagree

Question Number: 3

Which of the following words refers to half of the globe?

Ⓐ longitude
Ⓑ hemisphere
Ⓒ parallel
Ⓓ latitude

Question Number: 4

The prefix 'sub' in submarine means:

Ⓐ back or again
Ⓑ above or extra
Ⓒ under or below
Ⓓ across or over

Question Number: 5

The prefix 'hyper' in hyperactive means:

Ⓐ within, into
Ⓑ over or excessive
Ⓒ lacking or without
Ⓓ out of or former

Question Number: 6

If biology is the study of life, which answer choice explains the meaning of the word _geology_?

Ⓐ appreciation for the earth
Ⓑ a science class
Ⓒ the study of the earth
Ⓓ the study of life

Question Number: 7

Which of the following does NOT contain an affix?

Ⓐ autograph
Ⓑ photograph
Ⓒ telegraph
Ⓓ graphing

Question Number: 8

Choose the Latin suffix in the word <u>nonlikable</u>.

Ⓐ non
Ⓑ like
Ⓒ kable
Ⓓ able

Question Number: 9

What is the Latin root of the word <u>retractable</u>

Ⓐ re
Ⓑ retract
Ⓒ tract
Ⓓ able

Question Number: 10

Which word contains the Greek root that means 'time'?

Ⓐ chronicle
Ⓑ democracy
Ⓒ metamorphic
Ⓓ phonetics

Online Resources: The Meaning of Words

URL	QR Code
http://lumoslearning.com/a/15133	

 Videos   Apps   Sample Questions

NOTES

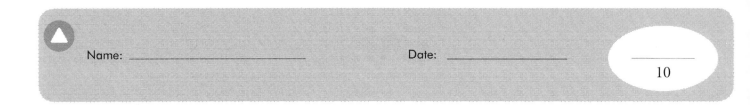
For Your Reference

Question Number: 1

Where would one look to find the definition of a key word when reading a science text-book?

- Ⓐ the glossary
- Ⓑ the thesaurus
- Ⓒ the dictionary
- Ⓓ the table of contents

Question Number: 2

Component. — N. component; component part, integral part, integrant part[obs3]; element, constituent, ingredient, leaven; part and parcel; contents; appurtenance; feature; member &c. (part) 51; personnel. V. enter into, enter into the composition of; be a component &c. n; be part of, form part of &c. 51; merge in, be merged in; be implicated in; share in &c. (participate) 778; belong to, appertain to; combine, inhere in, unite. form, make, constitute, compose. Adj. forming &c. v. inclusive.

What part of speech is the word, "component," in the thesaurus entry above?

- Ⓐ adjective
- Ⓑ verb
- Ⓒ adverb
- Ⓓ noun

Question Number: 3

Si-lently, adv. [f. SILENT a. + - LY ².]
    1. In a silent manner; without speaking, in
Silence ; without noise or commotion, noiselessly,
Quietly ; without mention or notice.
    1570-6 LAMBARDE *Peramb. Kent* (1826) 157. I could not
silently slip over such impieties. **1590** SHAKS. *Mids. N.* iii.
i. 206 Type vp my louers tongue, bring him silently. **1617**
MORYSON *Itin.* 1. 246 The Turkey company in London was
at this time..silently enjoying the safety and profit of this
trafficke. **1667** MILTON *P.L.* v. 130 She..silently a gentic
tear let fall. **1730** WATERLAND Rem. Clarke's Exp. Ch.
Catech. ii, What the compilers recommended chiefly to our
faith. he silently passes over. **1784** COWPER *Task* IV. 419
These ask with painful shyness, and refus'd Because deserv-
ing, silently retire! **1832** LYTTON *E. Aram* I. xi, Ellinor
silently made room for her cousin beside herself. **1878**
LECKY *Eng.* in 18th C.I. 313 Most of the..congregations
bad silently discarded the old doctrine of the Trinity.
    †2. Gradually, imperceptibly. Obs.⁻¹
    1668 CULPEPPER & COLE *Barthol. Anat.* I. xiii. 30 It goes
by little and little straight forward, and is silently termin-
ated towards the spleen.

How many definitions of "silently" are there in the dictionary entry above?

- Ⓐ 3   Ⓒ 1
- Ⓑ 4   Ⓓ 2

Question Number: 4

Veteran.— N. veteran, old man, seer, patriarch, graybeard; grandfather, grandsire; grandam; gaffer, gammer; crone; pantaloon; sexagenarian, octogenarian, nonagenarian, centenarian; old stager; dotard &c. 501. preadamite[obs3], Methuselah, Nestor, old Parr; elders; forefathers &c. (paternity) 166. Phr. "superfluous lags the veteran on the stage" [Johnson].

According to the thesaurus entry above, what is a synonym for the word, "veteran?"

Ⓐ veterinarian
Ⓑ graybeard
Ⓒ young man
Ⓓ None of the above

Question Number: 5

Skeletal (ske·l/tal), a. [f. SKELET-ON sb. +
-AL.] Of or belonging to, forming of formed by,
forming part of, or resembling, a skeleton.
  Skeletal muscle, a muscle attached to and controlling a
part of a skeleton.
  1854 OWEN in *Orr's Cire. Sci., Org. Nat. I.* 168 The
skeletal framework..does not go beyond the fibrous stage.
1872 HUMPHRY *Myology* 8 The skeletal formations in the
sternal region of the visceral wall. **1877** M. FOSTER *Physiol.*
I. ii. (1879) 37. All the ordinary striated skeletal muscles are
connected with nerves.

What is the definition of "skeletal?"

Ⓐ A bodily system made of muscle and bones, the most important systems in the body.
Ⓑ Made of bones
Ⓒ The skeletal region of the visceral wall
Ⓓ Of or belonging to, forming or formed by, forming part of, or resembling, a skeleton

Question Number: 6

Edge. — N. edge, verge, brink, brow, brim, margin, border, confine, skirt, rim, flange, side, mouth; jaws, chops, chaps, fauces; lip, muzzle. threshold, door, porch; portal &c. (opening) 260; coast, shore. frame, fringe, flounce, frill, list, trimming, edging, skirting, hem, selvedge, welt, furbelow, valance, gimp. Adj. border, marginal, skirting; labial, labiated[obs3], marginated[obs3].

Which of the following is NOT a synonym for "edge?"

Ⓐ brink
Ⓑ flank
Ⓒ verge
Ⓓ rim

Question Number: 7

Sitar (sitar). *Anglo-Ind.* Also sitarre. [Urdu
ستار *sitar.*] A form of guitar, properly having
three strings, used in India.
   1845 STOCQUELER *Hdbk. Brit. India* (1854) 26 A trio of
sitars, or rude violins. **1859** J. LANG *Wand. India* 152 Two
or three of the company..played alternately on the sitarre
(native guitar or violin). **1879** E. ARNOLD *f.t. Asia* VI. 144
One that twitched A three-string sitar. **1898** SIR G. ROBERT-
SON *Chitral* i. 7 A sitar-player will sing of love.
Sitarch.   *rare⁻°.*   [ad. Gr. oiTapxns or oiT-
apxos, f. oiTos corn, food.]   (See quots.)
   1656 BLOUNT *Glossogr.*, *Sitark*, he that hath the Office to
provide Corn, and Victuals sufficient. **1676** COLICS, *Starck*,
a Pourveyor.

Where might one see a sitar?

Ⓐ a hospital
Ⓑ a construction site
Ⓒ an international music festival
Ⓓ at the doctor's office.

Question Number: 8

Sky·scape. [f. SKY *sb.*[1] after *landscape*, seascape.] A view of the sky ; also in painting, etc., a representation of part of the sky.

1817 SOUTHEY *Let.* in *Life* (1850) IV. 283 It was the un-broken horizon which impressed me,..and the skyscapes which it afforded. **1861** C.J. ANDERSON Okavango x. 137 The beautiful and striking skyscapes and atmospheric coruscations attendant on these storms. 1878 GROSART *More's Poems* Introd. p. xii, The great ancient Painters, whose backgrounds of portraits..rather than land-scape, or sea-scape, or sky-scape proper, assure us [etc.]

Which of the following is not a meaning of the word, "skyscape?"

Ⓐ escaping by way of the sky
Ⓑ a view of the sky
Ⓒ a representation of part of the sky in painting, etc.
Ⓓ B & C

Question Number: 9

Notch. — N. notch, dent, nick, cut; indent, indentation; dimple. embrasure, battlement, machicolation[obs3]; saw, tooth, crenelle[obs3], scallop, scollop[obs3], vandyke; depression; jag. V. notch, nick, cut, dent, indent, jag, scarify, scotch, crimp, scallop, scollop[obs3], crenulate[obs3], vandyke. Adj. notched &c. v.; crenate[obs3], crenated[obs3]; dentate, dentated; denticulate, den-ticulated; toothed, palmated[obs3], serrated.

Which of the following synonyms for "notch" is a verb?

Ⓐ nick
Ⓑ embrasure
Ⓒ toothed
Ⓓ palmated

Question Number: 10

Slog (slog), v. colloq. [Of obscure origin. Cf. SLUG v.⁴]

1. *trans.* To hit or strike hard : to drive with blows. Also *fig.*, to assail violently.

1853 ˙ C.BEDE *Verdant Green* xi. 106 His whole person [had been] put in chancery, stung, bruised, fibbed,...slogged, and otherwise ill-treated. **1884** 'R. BOLDREWOOD' *Melb. Memories* iv. 32 We slogged the tired cattle round the fence. **1891** *Spectator* to Oct. 487/1 They love snubbing their friends and 'slogging' their enemies.

b. *Cricket.* To obtain (runs) by hard hitting.

1897 H. W. BLEAKLEY *Short innings* iii. 49 Mr. Dolly slogged sixes and fours until he had made about eighty.

2. *intr.* To walk heavily or doggedly.

Halliwell's ˙*Slog,* to lag behind' probably belongs to SLUGV.

1872 CALVERLEY *Fly Leaves (1903)* 119 Then abiit..off slogs boy. **1876** Mid-Yorksh. *Gloss., Slog,* to walk with burdened feet, as through snow, or puddle. **1907** Westm. Gaz. 2 Oct. 2/1 Overtaking the guns, we 'slogged' on with them for a mile or more.

3. To deal heavy blows, to work hard (at something), to labour away, etc.

1888 *Daily News* 22 May 5/2, I slogged at it, day in and day out. **1894** HESLOP *Northumberland Gloss.* s.v., They slogged away at the anchor shank. **1903** 19th Cent. Mar. 392 They have no incentives to slog and slave.

Which of the following is NOT a definition of the word, "slog?"

Ⓐ   to hit or strike hard
Ⓑ   to walk heavily or doggedly
Ⓒ   to deal heavy blows, to work hard
Ⓓ   to jump high and score

NOTES

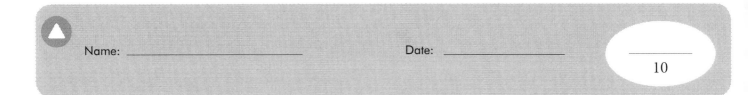
Similes and Metaphors

Question Number: 1

The sky was an angry, purple monster. It roared fiercely as the thunder crashed and rain poured down.

What does the metaphor in the first sentence mean?

Ⓐ The sky had clouds in the shape of a monster.
Ⓑ The sky was stormy.
Ⓒ Monsters invaded the town.
Ⓓ None of the above

Question Number: 2

In the days after Dad was laid off almost everyone was gloomy. Sam didn't smile, <u>Mom hovered over everyone like a cloud full of rain</u>. It was Sasha who was the ray of sunshine when she declared, "It's alright. Hugs are free!"

What purpose does the author's simile serve in the paragraph?

Ⓐ It describes the setting after Dad was laid off.
Ⓑ It makes the point that mom was gloomy and likely to cry.
Ⓒ It shows that Sasha was a happy, upbeat presence in the house.
Ⓓ It reminds us that hugs are free.

Question Number: 3

The starting goalie was out with an injury, so Kevin was finally getting his chance to prove his worth. He knew he could do it. He was ready. Kevin was a brick wall.

By comparing Kevin to a brick wall, what is the speaker trying to say about Kevin?

Ⓐ He would not allow anyone to score on him.
Ⓑ He was hard-headed.
Ⓒ He built a wall in front of his soccer goal.
Ⓓ He threw bricks at his opponent.

Question Number: 4

In the days after Dad was laid off almost everyone was gloomy. Sam didn't smile, Mom hovered over everyone like a cloud full of rain. <u>It was Sasha who was the ray of sunshine when she declared, "It's alright. Hugs are free!"</u>

What purpose does the author's metaphor serve in the paragraph?

Ⓐ It describes the setting after Dad was laid off.
Ⓑ It makes the point that mom was a gloomy and likely to cry.
Ⓒ It shows that Sasha was a happy, upbeat presence in the house.
Ⓓ It reminds us that hugs are free.

Question Number: 5

<u>Their family was like a patchwork quilt</u> of nationalities and colors. Each adopted child added something beautiful to the whole.

What does the simile in the above paragraph mean?

Ⓐ Like a patchwork quilt, the family was old and ragged. It was probably time to throw it out.
Ⓑ Their family had old-fashioned traditions, like a patchwork quilt from generations past.
Ⓒ Like a patchwork quilt, the children were adopted by parents who loved them very much.
Ⓓ Like a patchwork quilt that has bits of different fabric stitched together, the family had children of different nationalities and colors bound together as brothers and sisters. The overall effect was beautiful.

Question Number: 6

The ballerinas were like swans gliding over the stage.
Why does the speaker compare ballerinas to swans?

Ⓐ to show that they were white
Ⓑ to show that they squawked like birds
Ⓒ to show that they can swim
Ⓓ to show that they are graceful and elegant

Question Number: 7

Which similes below would be helpful in describing a terrified look on someone's face?

Ⓐ Her eyes drooped like wilted flowers, and her hands hung limp like wet spaghetti noodles.
Ⓑ Her eyes were as sharp as arrows, and her fists clenched tight like hammers waiting to strike.
Ⓒ Her eyes were soft like a morning dew, and her hands lay still as resting cherubs.
Ⓓ Her eyes were as big as sewer lids, and her hands trembled like tiny earthquakes.

Question Number: 8

Which metaphor below would be helpful in describing a presentation that went terribly?

Ⓐ In that moment Alfonso was a lion tamer, and the crowd was a well-trained pride eating from the palm of his hand.
Ⓑ In that moment Alfonso was the conductor of a train that was steady on its rails and going full steam ahead.
Ⓒ In that moment Alfonso was a bright flame, and the people gathered like moths around him.
Ⓓ In that moment Alfonso was the captain of an ill-fated voyage, and he was going dow with his ship.

Question Number: 9

Which simile below would help describe a child's joy in being reunited with a mother returning from a military tour of duty in another country?

Ⓐ Hannah's face lit up like fireworks on the Fourth of July when she glimpsed her mother rounding the corner. It was really her!
Ⓑ Hannah closed up like a locked bedroom door when she saw her mother for the first time.
Ⓒ Hannah pounded her fist on the counter like it was a judge's ruinous gavel when she saw her mother rounding the corner.
Ⓓ Hannah's eyes turned down, and her face turned red as a beet when she glimpsed her mother for the first time.

Question Number: 10

Which metaphor below would be helpful in describing a huge crowd of people at a festival?

Ⓐ The people marched through the streets with purpose, like an army marching toward battle.
Ⓑ The streets were a barren desert, and the music echoed off of empty storefronts.
Ⓒ A sea of delighted people swept over the sidewalks and into the street as they passed from attraction to attraction.
Ⓓ I was on an emotional roller coaster on the day of the festival.

NOTES

Idiomatic Expressions and Proverbs

Question Number: 1

If Wendy's dad found out she took her cell phone to school, he would _hit the ceiling_.

What is meant by the idiom _hit the ceiling_ in the above sentence?

Ⓐ Wendy's dad will jump high.
Ⓑ Wendy's dad will be very angry.
Ⓒ Wendy's dad will laugh loudly.
Ⓓ Wendy's dad will congratulate her.

Question Number: 2

I think you need to swallow your pride and apologize to your teacher for talking in class.

What is meant by the idiom swallow your pride?

Ⓐ to swallow hard
Ⓑ to deny doing something
Ⓒ to forget about being embarrassed
Ⓓ to pretend you are sorry

Question Number: 3

Mindy was walking on air after she went backstage and met Adam Levine.

What does the idiom 'walking on air' mean?

Ⓐ Mindy was floating through the air.
Ⓑ Mindy was dreaming.
Ⓒ Mindy was in a state of bliss.
Ⓓ Mindy was disappointed.

Question Number: 4

I am not sure how long I will stay at the dance. I'm going to play it by ear.

What is the meaning of '_play it by ear_' in the above sentence?

Ⓐ Play a musical instrument without sheet music.
Ⓑ Decide as you see how things go rather than making plans.
Ⓒ Listen for someone to tell you what to do.
Ⓓ Think carefully before making a decision.

Question Number: 5

After winning a million dollars, Kelly was running around like a chicken with its head cut off.

What does the idiom 'like a chicken with its head cut off' mean?

Ⓐ to act in a calm manner
Ⓑ to be bleeding profusely
Ⓒ to run around clucking and flapping your arms
Ⓓ to act in a frenzied manner

Question Number: 6

Jackie was not very happy. Not only did she lose her favorite necklace, but she also learned that her best friend was going to sleep-away camp for the whole summer while she had to go to summer school. Jackie really felt down in the dumps.

What does "down in the dumps mean" in the sentence?

Ⓐ sad
Ⓑ bringing the garbage to the end of the driveway
Ⓒ excited
Ⓓ flabbergasted

Question Number: 7

Amy's aunt spent months knitting a scarf for Amy. When Amy received the present and looked at it, she really didn't like the colors. She couldn't let her aunt know she was disappointed after all her hard work, so she told a little white lie instead.

What does a "little white lie" mean in the sentence?

Ⓐ huge made up story
Ⓑ truth
Ⓒ lie that is told to avoid hurting someone's feelings
Ⓓ the lie was painted white

Question Number: 8

The renovations the Johnsons were making on the house were getting too expensive. The Johnsons wanted the best of the best, but they didn't have enough money to pay for it all. Their architect came to speak with them. "You have some great ideas, but we're going to need to see where we can cut corners. We may have to change some of the original plans to save some money; otherwise we won't be able to finish the house."

What does "cut corners" mean in the sentence?

Ⓐ cut the edges of the play's program
Ⓑ clip some coupons
Ⓒ use money wisely and try to save by spending only what is necessary
Ⓓ mow the lawn

Question Number: 9

What does the idiom "Half a loaf is better than none" mean?

Ⓐ You can't judge a person's character by how he or she looks.
Ⓑ You usually do better than others if you get there ahead of others.
Ⓒ This means having something is better than not having anything at all.
Ⓓ Mind your own business and let others mind theirs.

Question Number: 10

What does the idiom "Beauty is only skin deep" mean?

Ⓐ If something unfortunate happens, it usually won't happen again.
Ⓑ Take care of a small problem before it becomes a big one.
Ⓒ A picture can explain things better than words.
Ⓓ You can't judge a person's character by how he or she looks.

Online Resources: Idiomatic Expressions and Proverbs

URL	QR Code
http://lumoslearning.com/a/15134	

 Videos   Apps   📖 Sample Questions

NOTES

Synonyms and Antonyms

Question Number: 1

Choose the correct set of synonyms for "_small_."

Ⓐ enormous, giant
Ⓑ minute, gargantuan
Ⓒ small, unseen
Ⓓ miniature, minute

Question Number: 2

Choose the correct set of _synonyms_.

Ⓐ unrealistic, believable
Ⓑ noteworthy, important
Ⓒ noteworthy, insignificant
Ⓓ unfair, just

Question Number: 3

Choose the correct set of _antonyms_.

Ⓐ radiant, dull
Ⓑ rescue, save
Ⓒ chortle, laugh
Ⓓ sparkle, shine

Question Number: 4

Choose the synonym for "_happy_."

Ⓐ miserable
Ⓑ ecstatic
Ⓒ subdued
Ⓓ wretched

Question Number: 5

Choose the correct set of antonyms for *"pretty."*

Ⓐ repulsive, unattractive
Ⓑ lovely, handsome
Ⓒ enticing, glamour
Ⓓ appealing, grotesque

Question Number: 6

What is a synonym for the word, "chaos?"

Ⓐ huge
Ⓑ agree
Ⓒ disorder
Ⓓ famous

Question Number: 7

Find the correct set of synonyms below.

Ⓐ fat and aged
Ⓑ tend and thick
Ⓒ fat and thick
Ⓓ aged and tend

Question Number: 8

Find the correct set of antonyms below.

Ⓐ peculiar and general
Ⓑ peculiar and common
Ⓒ general and included
Ⓓ general and common

Question Number: 9

What would be a good antonym for the word, "recall?"

Ⓐ contend
Ⓑ assert
Ⓒ forget
Ⓓ urge

Question Number: 10

What is an antonym for the word, "active?"

Ⓐ lazy
Ⓑ energetic
Ⓒ healthy
Ⓓ running

Online Resources: Synonyms and Antonyms

URL	QR Code
http://lumoslearning.com/a/15135	

 Videos   Apps   Sample Questions

NOTES

Academic and Domain Specific 4th Grade Words

Question Number: 1

When Jeremy arrived home his mom _____ him about the dance until he could think of no more details to give her.

Choose the word that best completes the sentence.

Ⓐ yelled at
Ⓑ quizzed
Ⓒ praised
Ⓓ waddled

Question Number: 2

The woodlands of the midatlantic region are filled with all sorts of interesting _____ .
Choose the word that best completes the sentence.

Ⓐ movies
Ⓑ wildlife
Ⓒ colleges
Ⓓ mortar

Question Number: 3

_____ John Muir helped preserve our country's natural beauty by helping to establish Yosemite National Park.

Choose the word that best completes sentence.

Ⓐ Antagoinist
Ⓑ Pianist
Ⓒ Conservationist
Ⓓ Statistician

Question Number: 4

Sarah was _____ at the news that the giant oak she had worked to protect was going to be removed in order to build a parking lot.

Choose the word that best completes the sentence.

Ⓐ crestfallen
Ⓑ starstruck
Ⓒ jovial
Ⓓ greedy

Question Number: 5

When an animal is _____ the government will sometimes place restrictions on hunting it.

Choose the word that best completes the sentence.

Ⓐ rabid
Ⓑ thretening
Ⓒ special
Ⓓ endangered

Question Number: 6

"Mommmmm, do I haaaaaave to?" Lester _____ as his mother sat across the table with her eyes trained on his Brussels sprouts.

Choose the word that best completes the sentence.

Ⓐ said
Ⓑ called
Ⓒ shrieked
Ⓓ whined

Question Number: 7

"Wha-wha-what was th-that?" Dera _____ as she climbed the creaky stairs in the old house.

Choose the word that best completes the sentence.

Ⓐ commanded
Ⓑ announced
Ⓒ stammered
Ⓓ laughed

Question Number: 8

My _____ is that the celery's stalk turned blue because it absorbed the colored water in the vase.

Ⓐ idea
Ⓑ intuition
Ⓒ guess
Ⓓ hypothesis

Question Number: 9

Monica _____ Peter's reasoning by referring to an example in the text that did not support the idea he suggested.

Ⓐ agreed
Ⓑ dissed
Ⓒ critiqued
Ⓓ slammed

Question Number: 10

When putting forth an idea about what a character is thinking, it is best to use _____ from the text.

Choose the word that best completes the sentence.

Ⓐ characters
Ⓑ evidence
Ⓒ chapters
Ⓓ nonfiction

End of Language

NOTES

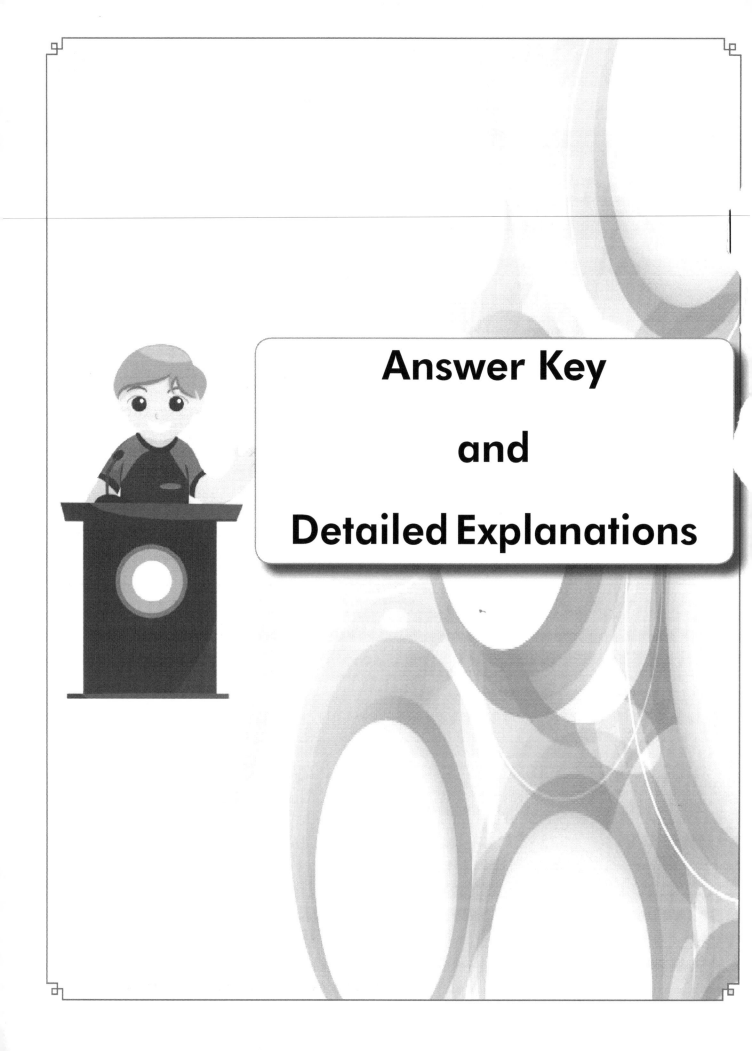

Answer Key

and

Detailed Explanations

Synonyms and Antonyms

Question No.	Answer	Detailed Explanation
1	D	"Miniature" and "minute" are synonyms of "small." Synonyms are words that mean the same thing.
2	B	"Noteworthy" and "important" are synonyms, or words that mean the same.
3	A	"Radiant" and "dull" are antonyms, or words that mean the opposite.
4	B	"Ecstatic" and "happy" are synonyms, or words that mean the same.
5	A	"Repulsive" and "unattractive" are antonyms for "pretty." Antonyms are words that mean the opposite.
6	C	"Chaos" and "disorder" are synonyms, or words that mean the same.
7	C	"Fat" and "thick" are synonyms, or words that mean the same.
8	B	"Peculiar" and "common" are antonyms, or words that mean the opposite.
9	C	"Recall" and "forget" are antonyms, or words that mean the opposite.
10	A	"Active" and "lazy" are antonyms, or words that mean the opposite.

Academic and Domain Specific 4th Grade Words

Question No.	Answer	Detailed Explanation
1	B	"Quizzed" makes the most sense in the sentence. It means she questioned him for details about the dance.
2	B	"Wildlife," meaning plants and animals, is the best choice. None of the other answer choices make sense.
3	C	"Conservationist," meaning someone who works to preserve wildlife, is the best choice here. The other choices make no sense in the sentence.
4	A	"Crestfallen," meaning disappointed, is the best choice to describe Sarah's emotion. The other choices do not make sense.
5	D	"Endangered," meaning in danger of becoming extinct, is the best choice. The other choices do not make sense in the sentence.
6	D	Although "said," "called," and "shrieked," are all verbs that could convey how a person spoke to another person, "whined" is the best fit in this sentence.
7	C	"Stammered," meaning stuttered, is the best word for the sentence.
8	D	"Hypothesis" is the best fit for the sentence. Scientists make hypotheses based on the evidence they have in order to explain an event.
9	C	"Critiqued," meaning evaluated or criticized, is the best fit for the sentence. "Agreed," does not make sense, and the other two choices are not fit to use in an academic context.
10	B	"Evidence" is the best choice for the sentence. The other words are related to reading but do not make sense in the sentence.

Common Core Standards Cross-reference Table

CCSS	Standard Description	Page No.	Question No.
L.4.1.A	Use relative pronouns (who, whose, whom, which, that) and relative adverbs (where, when, why).	8	1 to 10
L.4.1.B	Form and use the progressive (e.g., I was walking; I am walking; I will be walking) verb tenses.	13	1 to 10
L.4.1.C	Use modal auxiliaries (e.g., can, may, must) to convey various conditions.	17	1 to 10
L.4.1.D	Order adjectives within sentences according to conventional patterns (e.g., a small red bag rather than a red small bag).	22	1 to 10
L.4.1.E	Form and use prepositional phrases.	27	1 to 10
L.4.1.F	Produce complete sentences, recognizing and correcting inappropriate fragments and run-ons	31	1 to 10
L.4.1.G	Correctly use frequently confused words (e.g., to, too, two; there, their).	36	1 to 10
L.4.2.A	Use correct capitalization.	40	1 to 10
L.4.2.B	Use commas and quotation marks to mark direct speech and quotations from a text.	45	1 to 10
L.4.2.C	Use a comma before a coordinating conjunction in a compound sentence.		
L.4.2.D	Spell grade-appropriate words correctly, consulting references as needed.	49	1 to 10
L.4.3.A	Choose words and phrases to convey ideas precisely.	53	1 to 10
L.4.3.B	Choose punctuation for effect.	57	1 to 10
L.4.3.C	Differentiate between contexts that call for formal English (e.g., presenting ideas) and situations where informal discourse is appropriate (e.g., small-group discussion).	61	1 to 10
L.4.4.A	Use context (e.g., definitions, examples, or restatements in text) as a clue to the meaning of a word or phrase.	66	1 to 10
L.4.4.B	Use common, grade-appropriate Greek and Latin affixes and roots as clues to the meaning of a word (e.g., telegraph, photograph, autograph).	71	1 to 10
L.4.4.C	Consult reference materials (e.g., dictionaries, glossaries, thesauruses), both print and digital, to find the pronunciation and determine or clarify the precise meaning of key words and phrases.	75	1 to 10

CCSS	Standard Description	Page No.	Question No.
L.4.5.A	Explain the meaning of simple similes and metaphors (e.g., as pretty as a picture) in context.	81	1 to 10
L.4.5.B	Recognize and explain the meaning of common idioms, adages, and proverbs.	86	1 to 10
L.4.5.C	Demonstrate understanding of words by relating them to their opposites (antonyms) and to words with similar but not identical meanings (synonyms).	91	1 to 10
L.4.6	Acquire and use accurately grade-appropriate general academic and domain-specific words and phrases, including those that signal precise actions, emotions, or states of being (e.g., quizzed, whined, stammered) and that are basic to a particular topic (e.g., wildlife, conservation, and endangered when discussing animal preservation).	95	1 to 10

 **lumos learning**
Developed by Expert Teachers

Test Prep and Smart Homework Help

Lumos StepUp is a unique e-Learning program that provides online resources along with personalized coaching to help improve student achievement.

 Practice Assessments that mirror standardized Tests

 Parent Portal: Review online work of your child

 Individualized homework assistance (StepUp® Coach™)

 Student Portal: Anywhere access to Learning Resources

 15 Master Tech Enhanced Question Types

 Discover Educational Apps, Books, and Videos

Subscribe Now ▶

 888-309-8227

 www.lumoslearning.com/stepup

School Supplemental Program

COMPUTER-BASED SKILLS PRACTICE
AND ASSESSMENT REHEARSAL

➤ Standards-aligned workbooks

➤ Practice tests that mirror state assessments

➤ Fifteen tech-enhanced items practice

➤ Resource recommendations such as apps, books, & videos

➤ Personalized learning assignments for students

Call us for more information

888 - 309 - 8227

lumoslearning.com/a/online-program

Trusted by over 60,000 Students, 600 Schools, & 6000 Teachers

PARTIAL CUSTOMER LIST

Other Books in SkillBuilder Series

Reading Comprehension SkillBuilder

- Literature
- Informational Text
- Evidence-based Reading

Operations and Algebraic Thinking SkillBuilder

- Real World Problems
- Multi-Step Problems

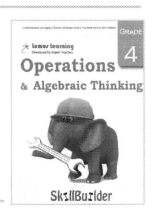

Fractions and Base Ten SkillBuilder

- Place Value
- Compare Numbers
- Compare Fractions

Measurement, Representation, Interpretation and Geometry SkillBuilder

- Units of Measurement
- Angle Measurement
- Classifying Plane

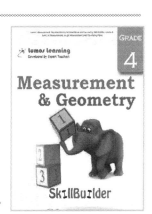

http://lumoslearning.com/a/sbtb

Made in the USA
Middletown, DE
18 April 2017